simply
Down Home
Cooking

Project Editor: Lisa M. Tooker
Editor: Ann Beman
Layout & Production: Patty Holden
Photography & Recipes: Lisa Keenan

Printed in China

ISBN: 1-59637-054-8

Table of Contents

The World of Down Home Cooking

In an ideal world, where the pace of life is slower and demands on time are fewer, you might imagine the ideal meal. You might imagine a repast made from fresh local produce and succulent meats that have been seasoned and cooked for as long as it takes to draw out their finest flavors and textures. The entire family and perhaps a few friends sit together at the splendidly set table, talking, laughing, and passing dish after home-cooked side dish, until finally, the main course arrives, inspiring, an awed hush.

In the real world, the daily demands on time are too great for such an occasion to be an everyday affair. Simply Down Home is designed to take advantage of today's conveniently prepared-yet-wholesome meats so that homecooks can create awe-inspiring meals—each and every day—with minimal time and effort.

But, you ask, why offer a cookbook that features already "fully cooked" products? Because these products are building blocks to quick-yet-fabulous meals that tower over the alternatives—expensive and often unwholesome fast food, or dishes so labor-intensive that the harried cook collapses with exhaustion before being able to put anything on the table.

As you will discover, these dishes, with their slightly Southwestern attitude, are imaginative, delicious, contemporary, and—best of all—easy. They call for simple ingredients, and yield spectacular results in a short period of time.

We encourage homecooks to take these recipes "down home," making them their own, with slight or grand variations. Variety, after all, is a crucial ingredient.

Basics

Remember: You don't always need to run to the grocery store. Think about what you have on your kitchen shelf—if you have the basics above, then you can quickly create most dishes at home quickly. When you run out of time to stop off at the store or guests stop by last minute, it's always reassuring to know that your pantry is stocked with what you will need to prepare a great meal at home.

It's easiest if you make a wish list with some of the items listed above, picking up things each time you shop, rather than gathering everything at once. Buying quality ingredients is also the key to success in the pantry; just remember to restock when ingredients run low. Once you have everything on hand, then cooking will be easy and quick every time—and you can enjoy the meal, rather than fuss over any last minute details.

Must-Have Basics

Baking powder and baking soda

Basil, cinnamon, crushed red pepper, nutmeg, oregano, paprika, parsley, pepper, rosemary, salt, and any of your favorite dried herbs

Beans, canned or dried and tuna

Bread, bread crumbs, and cornmeal

Cereals and oatmeal

Chocolate and cocoa

Coffee

Cornstarch, flour, rice, dry pasta

Dried fruits, nuts, and seeds

Garlic

Honey

Instant broths and sauces

Jams and jellies and canned fruit

Ketchup, tomato puree, and mustard

Milk

Oil

Olives and pickles

Pesto

Potatoes and onions

Raisins

Salsas and hot sauces

Soy and other Asian specialty sauces

Sugar

Syrup

Vanilla

Vinegars

High-End Basics

Cake mixes, cookies, and crackers

Capers

Chutney and other favorite specialty sauces

Dijon-style mustards

Dried chiles, cumin, cloves, cayenne pepper, ground ginger, marjoram

Dried mushrooms

Espresso

Horseradish, anchovy paste, and canned anchovies

Risotto rice (Arborio, basmati, brown, long-grain)

Sherry, cognac, and cooking wines

Specialty oils and vinegars

Sun-dried tomatoes

Tabasco, Worcestershire, and hot sauces

Yeast

Starters

Appetizers are meant to be served before a meal to whet and excite the palate. Often, these tastebud-ticklers are artfully prepared finger foods that travel directly from serving platter to guest's mouth. Other times, these little snacks are just that, "snacks," for hungry family members needing a little between-meal sustenance, or a light meal in itself. Whether you are serving the following recipes to party guests or to overscheduled teenagers, your home-cooked artistry will garner praise.

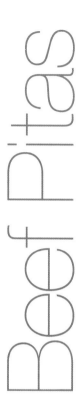

Beef Pitas

Serves 5:

12 ounces frozen, fully-cooked beef fajita strips
½ cucumber
½ small red onion
⅓ cup prepared balsamic vinaigrette dressing
5 pita flat bread
8 ounces regular cream cheese spread
4 ounces feta cheese crumbles
½ cup shredded mozzarella cheese
Plain yogurt, for garnish (optional)

Prep Time: 20 minutes
Cooking Time: 10 minutes

Clean and cut cucumber lengthwise in half and then crosswise into very thin slices. Cut onion into thin slices. Combine cucumber with onion and vinaigrette in a bowl. Set aside cucumber-onion mixture to blend flavors.

Warm fajitas strips in microwaveable dish, according to package instructions, and cut chicken into bite-sized pieces.

Cut each pita bread horizontally, forming a top and bottom. Lay cut-sides up and spread each pita with cream cheese. Sprinkle each with feta cheese, add cucumber-onion mixture over feta, and sprinkle top with mozzarella cheese. Place top of each pita with remaining halves, cut-sides facing down.

Bring 2 medium non-stick skillets to medium heat. Place 1 pita in each skillet; heat 2–3 minutes per side, until bread is browned and filling is cooked. Remove from skillet and heat remaining pitas as instructed above. Cut pita into wedges, serve with any remaining cucumber-onion mixture, and garnish with yogurt, if desired.

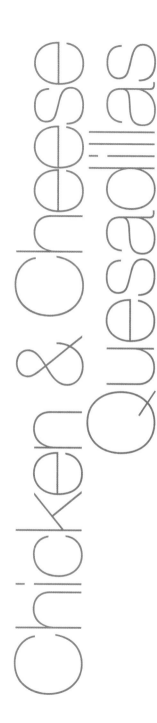

Chicken & Cheese Quesadillas

Serves 4:

12 ounces frozen, fully-cooked chicken fajita strips
½ red onion
3 ounces Parmigiano-Reggiano cheese
1 tablespoon oil
5–6 ounces fresh baby spinach leaves
Salt (preferably kosher or sea)
Freshly ground black pepper
Non-stick cooking spray
8 flour tortillas (6-inch)

Prep Time: 15 minutes
Cooking Time: 10 minutes

Warm chicken fajita strips in microwave, according to package directions.

Peel and cut onion in half and then slice very thinly. Grate Parmigiano-Reggiano cheese. Cut chicken fajitas into small chunks.

Over medium-high heat, heat oil in a large non-stick skillet, add onion, and sauté for 5 minutes or until onion is translucent. Add spinach to skillet and cook for an additional 30–60 seconds until spinach is wilted. Season with salt and pepper, as desired, remove from onion-spinach mixture from skillet, and set aside on a plate for later use.

Using the same skillet, spray with non-stick cooking spray. Cook 1 tortilla at a time, sprinkling each with 1 tablespoon cheese, and spread one-fourth fajita mixture and one-fourth spinach mixture over cheese. Top with 1 more tablespoon cheese and place second tortilla over top. Press down gently on tortilla and spray top of tortilla with non-stick spray. Flip tortilla over and brown other side. If skillet gets too hot, reduce heat or remove skillet from burner briefly. Continue with other tortillas, heating each side for about 2 minutes or until brown and cheese is melted. Cut tortillas into wedges and serve.

Serves 4:

12 ounces fully-cooked Mexican-seasoned shredded chicken
1 small bag tortilla chips
1 can pinto or black beans, rinsed and drained
2 cups shredded cheddar cheese
Jalapeño slices (optional)
Guacamole (optional)
Sour cream (optional)

Prep Time: 10 minutes
Baking Time: 10 minutes

Preheat oven to 375°F.

On a large baking sheet with sides, arrange tortilla chips evenly. Spread chicken shreds over chips, followed by pinto or black beans. Add cheddar cheese and jalapeño slices, if desired, over top.

Bake for 10–15 minutes, or until cheese is melted and bubbly. Place nachos on a platter and serve with guacamole and sour cream, if desired.

Spicy Chicken Nachos

Asian-Style Beef Wraps

Serves 4 (3 wraps per guest):

12 ounces frozen, fully-cooked ground beef crumbles
½ cup hoisin sauce
½ cup Asian-style peanut sauce
½ cucumber
½ cup shredded carrot
¼ cup chopped fresh mint leaves
12 large leaves Boston, Bibb, or butterhead lettuce
Fresh mint leaves, for garnish (optional)

Prep Time: 10 minutes
Cooking Time: 10 minutes

Cook beef crumbles in a large microwaveable dish, according to package directions.

Add hoisin and peanut sauces to beef crumbles, and microwave slightly to warm. Wash and chop cucumber. Add cucumber, carrots, and mint leaves to the beef, stirring mixture well.

Place equal amounts of beef mixture into the center of each lettuce leaf. Place fresh mint leaves on side of wraps for garnish, roll up, and serve.

Traditional Taco Dip

Serves 12:

12 ounces frozen, fully-cooked taco or Mexican-seasoned beef crumbles
2 cans refried beans (about 16 ounces each)
2 cups mashed avocado
Salt (preferably kosher or sea)
Freshly ground black pepper
1 cup refrigerated roasted-pepper salsa
2 cups sour cream
2 cups shredded Monterey Jack cheese
4 green onions with tops, chopped (about ½ cup)
Tortilla or corn chips (optional)

Prep Time: 15 minutes

Cook beef crumbles in microwave, according to package directions.

Evenly spread beans into bottom of a 9 by 13-inch pan, then add beef crumbles over beans. Follow with layering mashed avocado, salsa, and sour cream over beef. Sprinkle with cheese and green onions.

Serve taco dip with chips and enjoy!

Serves 8:

12 ounces frozen, fully-cooked taco or Mexican-seasoned beef crumbles
1 can refried beans
8 tostadas
1 avocado
Salt (preferably kosher or sea)
Freshly ground black pepper
Mild chunky salsa
⅓ cup sour cream
1 cup shredded Monterey Jack cheese

Prep Time: 10 minutes
Heating Time: 10 minutes

Preheat oven to 350°F.

Warm beef crumbles in microwave, according to package directions. Cook beans on a stovetop or heat in microwave until hot.

Bake tostadas on a large baking sheet in the oven for 5–10 minutes or until crispy and browned. Peel, remove pit, and mash avocado. Season avocado with salt and pepper as desired.

To make tortillas, spread refried beans on each, then add beef crumbles, and top with desired amount of salsa. Add avocado, dollop of sour cream, and sprinkle top with cheese. Serve warm.

Beef Tostadas

Baguette Slices with Beef and Mango Salsa

Serves 8–12:

Mango salsa:
1 mango
2 kiwi fruit
1 red bell pepper
½ bunch green onions with tops (about 3–4)
1 jalapeño pepper
¼ cup chopped fresh cilantro
2 tablespoons lime juice
Salt (preferably kosher or sea)
Horseradish sauce:
4 ounces cream cheese, softened
¼ cup horseradish
2 tablespoons mayonnaise
2 tablespoons Dijon mustard

1 pound fully-cooked beef tenderloin roast (or pot roast, if tenderloin not available)
1–2 loaves French baguette, thinly sliced

Prep Time: 25 minutes

MANGO SALSA: Seed, peel, and dice mango. Peel and dice kiwi, and remove seeds and stem and dice bell pepper. Chop green onions. Remove seeds and stem and mince jalapeño. Combine all ingredients together in a medium-sized bowl. Set aside to blend flavors, about 15–30 minutes.

HORSERADISH SAUCE: Blend together all ingredients in a separate, medium bowl until smooth and creamy. Set aside.

If serving immediately, cut tenderloin into about ⅛-inch-thick slices. If not ready to serve, then wrap beef slices in plastic wrap and place in refrigerator until ready to assemble.

To make appetizers, spread each bread slice with horseradish sauce, add 2–3 slices of beef, and top with 1–2 teaspoons horseradish sauce or amount as desired. Add mango salsa on top or serve on the side, and allow guests to place on the baguette slice as desired.

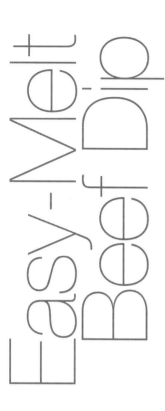

Easy-Melt Beef Dip

Serves 12–18:

12 ounces frozen, fully-cooked taco or Mexican-seasoned beef crumbles
2 pounds Velveeta (or other easy-melt cheese)
2 cans diced tomatoes and green chiles (about 10½ ounces each)
Tortilla or corn chips

Prep Time: 5 minutes
Cooking Time: 15 minutes

Heat beef crumbles in a large microwaveable dish, according to package directions.

Cut cheese into 1-inch-thick cubes.

Place cheese and diced tomatoes and green chiles with beef crumbles. Cover dish and heat in microwave on high for 8–10 minutes, stirring frequently while heating.

Ready to serve when cheese is melted and dip is hot. Serve with tortilla-style chips and eat quickly while still warm.

Serves 20–30 Appetizers:

4 ounces Parmesan cheese

Tomatoes:
1 ripe red tomato
1 ripe yellow tomato
2 tablespoons minced red onion
2 tablespoons finely chopped fresh basil
2 teaspoons red wine vinegar
¼ teaspoon salt (preferably kosher or sea)

1 loaf French baguette
4 cloves garlic, crushed
¼ cup olive oil
1½–2 pounds fully cooked beef tenderloin roast (or pot roast, if tenderloin not available)

Prep Time: 30 minutes
Broiling Time: 5 minutes

Slice Parmesan thinly and reserve for later use.

Chop red and yellow tomatoes finely. Toss tomatoes with onion, basil, vinegar, and salt. Set aside.

Heat oven to broil and place the oven rack 4–5 inches from broiler.

Cut baguette into ½-inch-thick slices and place on baking sheets. Combine garlic and oil and brush over tops of bread. Broil baguette slices for 1 minute on each side or until lightly browned. Remove from oven and reserve.

Cut tenderloin into ¼-inch-thick slices and then cut in half.

Top each reserved bread slice with about 1 tablespoon tomato mixture, 1 slice of beef, and a slice of Parmesan. Top each with a small amount of tomato mixture and broil for 1–2 minutes. Serve straight from the oven while still warm.

Bruschetta with Tomatoes and Beef

Salads and Soups

The word "salad" comes from the Latin words "herba salta" or "salted herbs," so called because such greens were usually seasoned with salt. The salad recipes that follow are about a lot more than seasoned herbs. They're meals in themselves, containing meats and a variety of veggies, herbs, and seasonings, tossed together with ease as well as style.

As early as 600 B.C., the Greeks sold soup as a fast food on the street. The soups in this section are fast, too, but unlike modern street fare, they're home-cooked and healthy. Together with crusty bread and/or your favorite tortillas and flatbreads, these meals in a bowl are substantial enough to satisfy hearty appetites.

Pasta Salad with Beef

Serves 4–6:

8 ounces tri-color rotini or fusilli pasta
12 ounces frozen, fully-cooked beef fajita strips
1 medium red bell pepper
4 ounces queso enchilado
½ cup chopped fresh cilantro
1 can black beans, drained and rinsed
1 can corn kernels, drained
¼ cup finely chopped red onion
Tortillas (optional)

Pasta dressing:
⅓ cup extra virgin olive oil
¼ cup lime juice
1 teaspoon salt (preferably kosher or sea)
½ teaspoon freshly ground black pepper

Prep Time: 15 minutes
Cooking Time: 10 minutes

In a large stockpot, heat 10 cups of water and bring to a boil. Place pasta in boiling water and cook according to package directions or just until al dente. Drain pasta and keep warm.

Cook fajitas, according to package directions and then cut into bite-sized pieces. Stir pasta dressing ingredients together in a small bowl using a whisk.

In a large bowl, combine pasta, beef fajitas, and pasta dressing together. Set aside for 5–10 minutes to blend flavors.

Chop bell pepper. Shred queso enchilado, including edges with seasoning.

Toss beans, corn, bell pepper, onion, cheese, and cilantro with pasta-beef fajita mixture. Best served immediately, if not, then keep in the refrigerator and serve cold when ready.

Tortillas served warm also go well as a side with this dish.

Crispy Taco Salad

Serves 4:

12 ounces frozen, fully-cooked beef or chicken fajita strips
1 large ripe tomato
1 large ripe avocado
1 cup coarsely crushed tortilla chips
16 ounces prepackaged salad mix (e.g., iceberg or romaine)
1 can black beans, rinsed and drained
1 cup shredded Monterey Jack
1 small can sliced ripe olives, drained
Salad dressing:
½ cup sour cream
½ cup salsa

Prep Time: 15 minutes

Warm beef or chicken fajitas in microwave, according to package directions. Cut chicken into bite-sized pieces

Rinse and cut tomato into wedges. Peel, remove pit, and cut avocado into small wedges. Crush tortilla chips into small pieces and reserve.

In a large bowl, combine salad dressing ingredients and toss with salad greens, beans, tomato, avocado, cheese, and olives.

Add fajita strips to salad mixture and top with reserved tortilla chips. It is ready to serve.

Serves 4:

3 pieces frozen, fully-cooked seasoned chicken breasts
4 teaspoons sweet chile sauce (Asian markets and specialty stores)
½ seedless cucumber
4 cups thinly sliced Napa cabbage
½ cup sliced green onions (white and green parts)
2 cups thinly sliced carrots
1½ cups chow mein noodles
½–⅓ cup Asian-style salad dressing (from store-bought bottle)
Fresh baguette (optional)

Prep Time: 15 minutes

Cook chicken breasts in a microwaveable dish, according to package directions. Add sweet chile sauce to coat chicken and set aside.

Cut cucumber into thin, round slices. Cut chicken breasts into thin strips.

In a large bowl, combine cabbage, cucumber, green onions, carrots, and chow mein noodles with prepared dressing. Place chicken strips over top of mixture and serve immediately with fresh bread.

Chow Mein-Slaw with Chicken

Mexican Chicken Caesar Salad

Serves 4:

12 ounces frozen, fully-cooked chicken fajita strips
4 red or yellow corn tortillas
¼ cup oil
2 ripe mangos
1 head romaine lettuce
¼ cup grated queso cotija or fresh Parmesan cheese
Bread rolls (optional)
Salad dressing:
½ cup Caesar salad dressing (from store-bought bottle)
1 tablespoon grated queso cotija or fresh Parmesan cheese
2 tablespoons chopped fresh cilantro
1 tablespoon lime juice

Prep Time: 15 minutes
Cooking Time: 5 minutes

Cook fajitas in a microwaveable dish, according to package directions.

Combine salad dressing ingredients in a medium bowl and reserve.

Cut tortillas into ½-inch wide by 2-inch long strips. Over medium-high heat, heat oil in a medium-sized skillet. Place chicken fajita strips in oil, spreading evenly. Cook about 2 minutes on each side, turning with a spatula. Place chicken on paper towels to drain and reserve.

Peel, remove seeds, and cut each mango into small wedges.

Wash and tear romaine lettuce into bite-size pieces. Toss lettuce with dressing in a large bowl. Place chicken fajita strips, mango wedges, and tortilla strips over top. Sprinkle with cheese and serve. Salad goes well with fresh, hot bread rolls

Mango and Chicken Salad

Serves 4–6:

¼ cup sweet chile sauce (Asian markets and specialty stores)
2 tablespoons chicken broth
2–3 pieces frozen, fully-cooked chicken breasts
2 ripe mangoes
½ red onion
12 ounces packaged herb-salad mix
6 ounces fresh baby spinach
¼ cup roasted and salted sunflower kernels

Sweet dressing:
2 tablespoons vegetable oil
2 tablespoons white wine vinegar
2 tablespoons frozen orange juice concentrate
1 tablespoon honey

Prep Time: 30 minutes

Over medium-high heat, add sweet chile sauce and broth in a small saucepan. Simmer until sauce thickens slightly, about 2 minutes, and remove saucepan from heat source.

Cook chicken breasts in a microwaveable dish, according to package directions. When chicken is cooked, cut into ¼-inch-wide by 2-inch-long strips. Combine chicken with sweet chile-broth sauce and let marinate.

Peel, remove seeds, and slice mangoes into cubes. Cut onion into thin rings.

SWEET DRESSING: Combine ingredients together in a large bowl. Add salad greens, mangoes, and onions to dressing and mix. Drain chicken strips from sauce and place over top of salad-mango mixture and sprinkle with sunflower kernels. Serve.

Serves 4:

2 pieces frozen, fully-cooked pesto- or Italian-seasoned chicken breasts
¼ cup pine nuts
½ head leaf lettuce
½ seedless cucumber
3 small ripe Roma tomatoes
⅓ cup coarsely chopped, pitted kalamata olives
5 ounces packaged salad mix
1 cup crumbled feta cheese
⅓ cup balsamic vinaigrette (from store-bought bottle)
Garlic bread (optional)

Prep Time: 15 minutes

Cook chicken breasts in a microwaveable dish, according to package directions.

Over medium heat, toast pine nuts, stirring frequently, in a small skillet for 3–4 minutes. Let cool and reserve.

Wash, spin-dry salad mix, and tear into bite-sized pieces. Cut cucumber into ¼-inch-thick slices and chop tomatoes.

In a large bowl, combine cucumber, tomatoes, and olives with balsamic dressing. Set aside. Chop chicken into bite-sized pieces.

Place salad in the bowl with vegetables and combine to coat evenly. Place chicken, pine nuts, and feta on top of chicken. Serve with hot garlic bread as a side.

Italian Chicken salad

Almond Chicken Salad

Serves 4–6:

2–3 pieces frozen, fully-cooked seasoned chicken breasts
½ cup slivered almonds
2 medium apples
1 cup finely chopped celery
⅓ cup chopped green onions
¼ cup currants
Boston or romaine lettuce leaves
Shredded coconut (optional)
Salad dressing:
⅓ cup mayonnaise
¼ cup mango chutney (prepared)
2 teaspoons lemon juice
2 teaspoons curry powder
½ teaspoon salt (preferably kosher or sea)
½ teaspoon freshly ground black pepper

Prep Time: 15 minutes

Cook chicken breasts in a microwaveable dish, according to package directions. When chicken is cooked, slice into ½-inch-thick cubes.

Over medium heat, toast almonds in a skillet for 2–3 minutes, stirring frequently, until golden. Reserve almonds.

Combine salad dressing ingredients in a small bowl and set aside.

Core apples and chop finely. Combine chicken, apple, celery, green onions, and currants in a large bowl. Add salad dressing to chicken mixture and combine, coating evenly.

Place lettuce leaves on each plate and spoon chicken salad mixture onto lettuce leaves. Sprinkle each plate with almonds and coconut, if desired.

Asparagus and Chicken Pasta Salad

Serves 4–6:

12 ounces penne rigate pasta
2–3 pieces frozen, fully-cooked Italian-seasoned chicken breasts
1 pound fresh asparagus
12–16 ounces fresh grape tomatoes
⅔ cup chopped fresh basil
½ cup pitted, coarsely chopped kalamata olives
1 cup crumbled feta (or ½ cup shredded Parmesan cheese)
Italian dressing:
¼ cup lemon juice
¼ cup balsamic vinegar
¼ cup extra virgin olive oil
1 teaspoon salt (preferably kosher or sea)
1 teaspoon freshly ground black pepper

Prep Time: 15 minutes
Cooking Time: 10 minutes

In a stockpot, bring about 3 quarts water to a boil and cook pasta according to package instructions or until al dente. Drain, keep warm, and reserve.

Cook chicken in a microwaveble dish, according to package directions. Remove and discard ends from asparagus. Slice asparagus into 1-inch pieces. Cook asparagus in a large skillet in shallow water and boil 1–2 minutes until crisp-tender. Drain well and reserve.

Chop chicken into 1-inch-thick pieces. Cut tomatoes in half. In a bowl, combine Italian dressing ingredients.

Add reserved pasta and asparagus to Italian dressing and coat evenly. Add chicken, tomatoes, basil, olives, and cheese and stir to combine. Pasta salad can be served warm or at room temperature.

Fried-Chicken and Tomato Salad

Serves 4:

2 pieces frozen, fully-cooked chicken-fried chicken breasts
24 ounces each iceberg salad blend (2 prepackaged bags)
2 cups cherry tomatoes
1 bunch green onions (white parts only)
½ seedless cucumber
4 radishes
Ranch salad dressing (from store-bought bottle)

Prep Time: 15 minutes

Cook chicken breasts in microwaveable dish, according to package directions.

Slice cherry tomatoes in half and chop green onions. Cut cucumber into ¼-inch-thick slices. Clean, dry, and slice radishes into thin slices.

Cut chicken breast into ½-inch-wide slices.

Combine salad with tomatoes, onions, cucumber, and radishes. Add ranch dressing and toss with salad to coat evenly. Arrange salad mixture on plates and top with chicken breast strips.

Serves 4–6:

1 medium onion
1 green bell pepper
1 tablespoon vegetable oil
1 packet chili seasoning mix (1.25 ounces)
1 can diced tomatoes (14½ ounces), undrained
12 ounces frozen, fully-cooked ground beef crumbles or taco-seasoned crumbles
1 can black beans
1 can corn, drained

Prep Time: 5 minutes
Cooking Time: 25 minutes

Remove skin and chop onion. Remove seeds, destem, and chop bell pepper.

Over medium-high heat, add oil to a large skillet and add onion and bell pepper. Sauté for 3 minutes and stir in chili seasoning, cooking for an additional minute. Add tomatoes with juice and beef. Bring mixture to a boil, then reduce heat to medium-low. Cover skillet and simmer for 10 minutes.

Drain and rinse beans. Add beans and corn to skillet with beef mixture. Add water until chili reaches semi-chunky consistency, about 1–1½ cups water. Simmer for an additional 5 more minutes. Serve while hot in bowls.

Chili con Carne

Rustic Corn and Chicken Stew

Serves 4–6:

1 onion
4 cloves garlic
1 cup finely chopped carrot
1 tablespoon oil
2 cups fresh or frozen corn kernels
2 cans chicken broth (14½ ounces each)
12 ounces shredded fully-cooked seasoned chicken
Salt (preferably kosher or sea)
Freshly ground black pepper
1 cup chopped ripe tomatoes
2 cups freshly grated Parmesan cheese
½ cup chopped fresh cilantro
Lime wedges (optional)
Chopped green onions (optional)

Prep Time: 10 minutes
Cooking Time: 15 minutes

Peel and chop onion and mince garlic.

Over medium-high heat, heat oil in large skillet and sauté onion and carrot until onion is translucent, about 5 minutes.

Add corn and garlic to skillet, and sauté for 3–5 minutes or until corn is golden and other vegetables are browned.

Add chicken broth to skillet and bring vegetable mixture to a boil. Add shredded chicken, stirring until chicken is heated. Season with salt and pepper to taste.

Serve stew in bowls and top with tomatoes, Parmesan, and cilantro. If desired, place lime wedges and green onions as condiments to serve with stew.

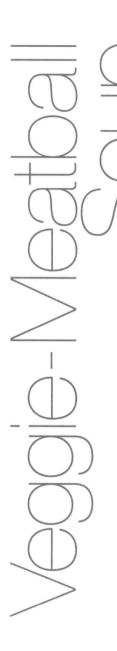

Veggie-Meatball Soup

Serves 4–6:

2 medium carrots
1 large onion
1 medium zucchini
1 tablespoon olive oil
2 cans white beans (15½ ounces each), undrained
1 can Italian-style stewed tomatoes (14½ ounces)
1 can beef broth (14½ ounces)
2 cups frozen, fully-cooked Italian-style meatballs
½ cup chopped fresh basil
1 teaspoon salt (preferably kosher or sea)
1 teaspoon freshly ground black pepper

Prep Time: 5 minutes
Cooking Time: 25 minutes

Wash, peel, and slice carrots thinly. Peel and chop onion. Cut ends and discard from zucchini, then cut into thin slices.

In a large saucepan over medium-high heat, heat oil and add carrots and onion, and sauté for 5 minutes. Add zucchini, beans, tomatoes, beef broth, and meatballs. Mix and bring vegetable-meatball mixture to a boil.

Cover saucepan, reduce heat to medium-low, and simmer for 15 minutes, stirring occasionally. Add basil, salt, and pepper to vegetable-meatball soup and cook for 2 more minutes. Ladle into soup bowls and serve hot.

Serves 8:

2 pounds fully-cooked beef pot roast with juices
2 cans beef broth (15½ ounces each)
1 can diced tomatoes (14½ ounces)
1 pound new potatoes (about 12–14)
2 medium zucchini
1 medium onion
1 teaspoon Tabasco
½ teaspoon dried thyme
½ teaspoon salt (preferably kosher or sea)
½ teaspoon freshly ground black pepper
1 can kidney beans, rinsed and drained
16 ounces frozen corn

Prep Time: 10 minutes
Cooking Time: 20 minutes

Over high heat, add pot roast juices to a large stockpot. Add beef broth and tomatoes and bring to a boil.

Cut potatoes into ½-inch-thick cubes, slice zucchini into ¼-inch-thick slices, and chop onion.

Place potatoes, zucchini, onion, Tabasco, thyme, salt, and pepper to stockpot. Bring all to a boil and then reduce heat to medium-low. Cover stockpot with lid and simmer for 10 minutes.

Cut pot roast into ½-inch cubes. Add pot roast, beans, and corn to stew. Cover again with lid and simmer for 5 more minutes. Ladle into large bowls and serve hot on a blustery day.

Winter Stew

Sandwiches Burgers, and Pizzas

Sandwiches have been around since the first century, B.C. But they weren't called "sandwiches" until the 1700s, when England's 4th Earl of Sandwich, reportedly too busy for a meal, ordered his valet to bring him meat tucked between two pieces of bread. Ever since, the world of sandwiches continues to evolve into toasted, broiled, and grilled masterpieces. And the sandwich's beefier cousin, the hamburger, gets noble treatment with humble preparations, calling for toppings from apples and blue cheese, to pineapple and honey barbecue sauce.

And, if you're in the mood for an Italian-inspired savory tart made with crisp yeast dough, covered with tomato sauce, try a slice of pizza. American has since made this creation her own, creating varieties such as deep-dish and thin-crust pies. In this section, we have both. Plus, meaty delicacies, easy-to-find jar sauces, and healthy toppings for down-home, fun-to-make pizzas.

Hawaiian Burgers

Serves 4:

4 frozen precooked cheeseburger patties (or 4 frozen hamburger patties topped with
    4 slices cheddar cheese)
1 package Canadian bacon (3½ ounces)
4 hamburger buns or Kaiser rolls
½ cup honey barbecue sauce
1 can pineapple slices (8 ounces), drained
Boston, Bibb, or leaf lettuce leaves
Red onion slices (optional)

Prep Time: 5 minutes
Heating Time: 5–10 minutes

Heat cheeseburgers in microwave, according to package directions. Arrange Canadian bacon slices on top of burgers, cover burgers with a paper towel, and reheat 20–30 seconds more in microwave.

Cut buns in half and toast. Spread barbeque sauce on one side of bun. Remove burgers from microwave, and place burgers, pineapple, lettuce, and red onion, if desired, to bottom bun. Place top bun on top and serve warm.

Serves 4:

½ cup refried beans
½ cup salsa
4 frozen, fully-cooked burger patties
4 hamburger buns or Kaiser rolls
Mayonnaise
Tomato slices
Lettuce leaves
1 small bag Fritos (½ cup), coarsely crushed

Prep Time: 5 minutes
Heating Time: 5 minutes

In a small bowl, combine beans and salsa. Spread bean-salsa mixture over each burger and place on a microwaveable plate. Cover and heat in microwave, according to package directions. Check burgers about halfway through heating time and rotate, if necessary.

Cut buns in half and toast. Spread mayonnaise on buns. Place bottom bun on serving plate, layer with tomato, lettuce, and burger, with bean-salsa facing upwards. Top with Fritos and press lightly so they stick to the beans. Cover with top bun and serve.

Burgers with Blue Cheese

Serves 4:

1 tart red apple
4 ounces blue cheese
4 Kaiser rolls or hamburger buns
4 frozen, fully-cooked burger patties
½ cup honey mustard
Leaf or romaine lettuce leaves
Red onion slices (optional)

Prep Time: 15 minutes
Grilling Time: 10 minutes

Prepare grill for barbecuing burgers.

Core and cut apple into 4 slices. Cut cheese into thin slices and slice rolls in half.

Grill should be heated between medium and high heat. Arrange frozen burgers on grill grate and heat 5 minutes on each side or until desired doneness. When burgers cooked on both sides, then lay cheese slices on burgers, followed by apples. Grill for 2–3 more minutes to melt cheese slightly. Remove burgers from grill, at the same time, place rolls on the outside edges of grill, toasting bread until golden.

Spread mustard on each half of roll. On bottom roll half, layer, burger, apple slice, lettuce, and onion, if desired. Top with roll top and serve right away while warm and juicy.

Spicy Burgers

Serves 4:

4 frozen, fully-cooked burger patties
½ small sweet onion
1 tablespoon butter
1 can whole green chiles (4 ounces), drained
4 slices Monterey Jack
4 hamburger buns
Salsa

Prep Time: 10 minutes
Heating Time: 5 minutes

Place burgers on a microwaveable platter and heat according to package directions.

Slice onion into ¼-inch-thick slices.

In a large frying pan over medium heat, add butter and sauté onion for 2–3 minutes, until translucent.

Cut green chiles in half and place on burgers, followed by 1 slice of cheese for each burger. Return to microwave and reheat for 1 minute or until cheese melts.

Toast each bun and add salsa over top.

Place burgers on bottom bun, top with sautéed onions, and cover with top bun. Serve immediately.

Serves 4–6:

16 ounces fully-cooked sliced Philly beefsteak
1 large loaf French or Italian bread
6 ounces cream cheese (softened or spreadable)
⅓ cup sour cream
¼ cup finely chopped fresh or canned jalapeño peppers
½ cup salsa
1½ cups shredded Monterey Jack cheese

Prep Time: 10 minutes
Heating Time: 15 minutes

Preheat oven to broil.

In a microwaveable dish, cook beefsteak in microwave, according to package directions.

Slice loaf in half and place each half, cut-side down, on a baking sheet. Place bread in oven on broil for 2 minutes or until lightly golden. Remove from oven and turn bread cut-side upward.

Mix together cream cheese, sour cream and peppers, and spread mixture on each loaf half. Place beefsteak slices over both halves of bread, lightly drizzle with salsa, and sprinkle with cheese.

Return sandwich to broiler and heat for about 2 minutes, or until cheese melts and top begins to brown. Let cool slightly and cut each loaf halve into 2–3 servings.

Open-Faced Beefsteak

Meatball Sandwich

Serves 4–6:

16 ounces frozen, fully-cooked Italian-style meatballs
2 cups pasta sauce (prepared)
1 medium green or red bell pepper
1 bunch green onions with tops, sliced
4 large French bread rolls (submarine-style)
½ cup shredded mozzarella cheese

Prep Time: 15 minutes
Heating Time: 5 minutes

Preheat oven to broil.

In a large microwaveable dish, place meatballs and pasta sauce and heat, according to package directions.

Remove seeds and stem from pepper and cut into very thin slices.

Cut rolls in half, leaving one edge attached like a hinge. Place rolls on a large baking sheet, cut-sides down. Toast in broiler for 1–2 minutes, or until lightly toasted.

Take rolls out of the oven and lay meatballs, reserving pasta sauce, over bottom side of roll. Add pepper and onion slices on top of meatballs, and top with pasta sauce. Sprinkle cheese over top and return to broiler for 1–2 minutes, or until cheese is melted. Remove and close down on top of roll and serve hot.

Chicken-Fried Steak Sandwich

Serves 4:

4 frozen, fully-cooked chicken-fried steaks
1 red or green bell pepper
4 large French bread rolls (submarine-style)
½ cup fresh salsa
½ cup ranch dip
Green or red leaf lettuce

Prep Time: 10 minutes
Cooking Time: 6 minutes

Preheat oven to broil.

Using a microwaveable dish, heat chicken-fried steaks in microwave, according to package directions. Remove stem and seeds from pepper, and slice very thinly.

Cut rolls in half, leaving one edge attached like a hinge. Place rolls, ·cut-side down, on a baking sheet and toast in broiler for 1–2 minutes or until lightly toasted.

In a small bowl, combine salsa and ranch dip. Spread salsa-ranch dip mixture on top and bottom side of each roll, then place peppers, lettuce, and chicken-fried steak onto bottom half of roll. Close down on top and serve warm.

Serves 4:

4 pieces frozen, fully-cooked chicken-fried chicken breasts
1 green bell pepper
1 loaf French bread
½ cup marinara sauce (prepared)
4 teaspoons grated Parmesan cheese
1 small can sliced ripe olives, drained
4 slices provolone cheese
Marinara sauce (prepared)

Prep Time: 15 minutes
Broiling Time: 5 minutes

Preheat oven to broil.

In a microwaveable dish, heat chicken breasts in microwave, according to package directions.

Remove stem and seeds from bell pepper and cut into ¼-inch-thick rings.

Slice bread loaf in half along center. Place bread halves, cut-sides down, on a baking sheet, and broil for about 2 minutes or until lightly browned.

Remove bread halves from oven, cut-side up. On bottom half, spread marinara sauce and sprinkle with Parmesan cheese. Place bell pepper rings, olives, and one slice of provolone over each.

Return bottom bread halve to broiler for about 2 minutes or until cheese melts. Remove from oven and place chicken on bottom half and firmly press top half together with bottom. Serve with heated marinara sauce on the side for dipping.

Italian Chicken Sandwiches

Hot Ciabatta with Chicken and Mushrooms

Serves 4:

2–3 pieces frozen, fully-cooked Italian-seasoned chicken breasts
1 medium sweet onion
4–6 ounces cremini mushrooms, sliced
2 tablespoons butter
½ cup dry Marsala wine
½ teaspoon freshly ground black pepper
4 ounces fontina cheese, thinly sliced
1 loaf ciabatta bread

Prep Time: 5 minutes
Cooking Time: 20 minutes

Preheat oven to broil.

In a microwableable dish, heat chicken breasts in microwave, according to package directions. Thinly slice chicken breasts and set aside.

Cut onion into thin slices.

In a large skillet over medium-high heat, add butter and sauté mushrooms and onion for 7–9 minutes or until tender. Add reserved chicken strips and wine to skillet. Season with black pepper and cook for 3–5 minutes or until wine is almost evaporated, stirring frequently.

Cut ciabatta in half along center. Place each ciabatta half on a baking sheet under broiler and toast each side for about 1–2 minutes.

Place chicken-mushroom mixture on bottom half of bread and sprinkle top with cheese. Place ciabatta bottom half in broiler to melt cheese, if desired. Place top half over bottom and press together gently. Cut ciabatta into 4 servings and eat.

Chicken Flat Bread Sandwiches

Makes 6 wraps:

12 ounces frozen, fully-cooked breaded popcorn chicken
2 cups shredded lettuce
1 cup diced tomatoes
6 pieces handmade Turkish flat breads
½ cup ranch dressing

Prep Time: 10 minutes
Heating Time: 12–16 minutes

Preheat oven to 425°F.

On a foil-lined baking sheet, place popcorn chicken evenly on the sheet. Cook for 6 – 8 minutes on each side or until chicken is golden brown and crispy on both sides.

In a frying pan over medium-high heat, fry each flat bread for 1 – 2 minutes per side. Keep bread warm in a bread basket.

Open flat bread and spread ranch dressing along sides. Arrange chicken evenly in the center and top with lettuce and tomatoes. Press firmly together to close the pocket. Serve hot.

Texas-Style Barbeque Pizza

Makes 2 pizzas:

2 Boboli thin pizza crusts (10 ounces each)
16 ounces fully-cooked sliced beef brisket with BBQ sauce
⅓–½ cup barbecue sauce
2 cups shredded Monterey Jack cheese
½ cup chopped red onion
½ cup chopped dill pickle

Prep Time: 15 minutes
Cooking Time: 15–20 minutes

Preheat oven to 450°F. Prepare oven racks by placing in bottom half of oven. Place pizza crusts on baking sheets or round pizza pans.

Add barbecue sauce from brisket package into a measuring cup. Add additional barbecue sauce to make 1 cup and stir to combine. Chop brisket slices coarsely.

Spread barbecue sauce evenly on each pizza crust. Arrange brisket over sauce. Sprinkle cheese, onion, and pickle over tops of pizzas.

Bake for 15–20 minutes, or until cheese melts and begins to brown. Rotate pans halfway through cooking on oven racks to ensure even browning. Let cool a few minutes and cut into slices and serve.

Makes 2 pizzas:

12 ounces fully-cooked seasoned shredded beef
2 Boboli thin pizza crusts (10 ounces each)
1½ cups salsa
4 cups shredded Colby Jack cheese, divided
1 can black beans, rinsed and drained
1 can whole green chiles

Prep Time: 10 minutes
Cooking Time: 15 minutes

Preheat oven to 450°F. Arrange 2 oven racks in bottom half of oven. Place crusts on baking sheets or round pizza pans.

Evenly distribute ¾ cup salsa and top with 1 cup cheese over each pizza.

Place shredded beef evenly over cheese and beans over beef.

Top each pizza with 1 cup of cheese. Slice chiles into thin strips and arrange over tops of pizzas.

Bake 15–20 minutes, or until cheese is melted. Switch pizzas on oven racks halfway through baking for even browning.

Allow pizzas to cool for a few minutes. Slice and serve.

Mexican Pizzas

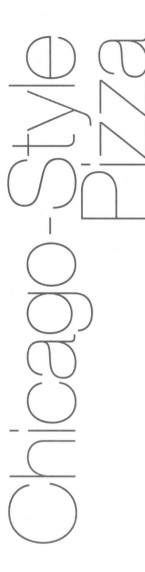

Chicago-Style Pizza

Serves 4–6:

12 ounces frozen, fully-cooked ground beef crumbles
1 box Chef Boyardee Pizza Kit (sauce and cheese included with kit)
1 tablespoon oil (for pizza kit)
2 cups shredded mozzarella or pizza-style cheeses
1 red or green bell pepper
1 can chopped black olives (2.25 ounce), drained
1 cup chopped green onions

Prep Time: 10–20 minutes
Cooking Time: 20 minutes

Preheat oven to 425°F. Cook beef crumbles in microwave according to package directions.

Prepare crust from pizza kit according to package directions. Let dough stand 5–20 minutes at room temperature. Wash bell pepper, remove seeds, and slice into rings.

Push dough evenly on bottom of a greased 9 by 13-inch baking dish. Spread 1 cup pizza sauce over dough, sprinkle with 1 cup shredded cheese, and beef crumbles over cheese. Layer with remaining pizza sauce, 1 cup cheese, and pizza kit cheese. Place bell pepper rings, olives, and green onions over top.

Bake 18–20 minutes, or until crust is golden brown. Remove from oven and let stand a few minutes before cutting. Slice into squares and serve while hot.

Basil, Chicken, and Tomato Pizzas

Makes 2 pizzas:

12 ounces frozen, fully-cooked chicken fajita strips
2 Boboli thin pizza crusts (10 ounces each)
2 Roma tomatoes
1½ cups Alfredo sauce (from a jar)
2 cups shredded mozzarella cheese
1 can mushroom stems and pieces, drained
¼ cup grated Parmesan cheese
Chopped fresh basil leaves (optional)

Prep Time: 10 minutes
Baking Time: 15 minutes

Preheat oven to 450°F. Arrange 2 oven racks in bottom half of oven. Place crusts on baking sheets or round pizza pans.

Heat chicken in microwave according to package directions. Chop chicken into bite-sized pieces and finely dice tomatoes.

Layer ¾ cup Alfredo sauce and 1 cup mozzarella cheese over each pizza crust. Place chicken, mushrooms, and tomatoes over sauce and cheese. Top with grated Parmesan.

Bake 15–20 minutes, or until cheese is melted. Switch pizzas on oven racks halfway through baking, if necessary for even browning. Allow pizzas to cool for a few minutes, slice, and serve. Top with fresh basil, if desired.

Makes 2 pizzas:

12 ounces fully-cooked seasoned shredded chicken
2 Boboli thin pizza crusts (10 ounces each)
1½ cups fire-roasted barbecue sauce
1 can pineapple tidbits (8 ounces), drained
½ cup chopped red onion
2 cups shredded mozzarella cheese

Prep Time: 10 minutes
Baking Time: 15 minutes

Preheat oven to 450°F. Arrange 2 oven racks in bottom half of oven. Place crusts on baking sheets or round pizza pans.

Cook chicken in microwave according to package directions.

Spread ¾ cup barbecue sauce over each crust. Arrange chicken, pineapple, and onion over pizzas. Top with cheese.

Bake 15–20 minutes, or until cheese melts. Switch pizzas on oven racks halfway through baking for even browning. Allow to cool for a few minutes, slice, and serve.

Fire-Roasted Pizzas

Mediterranean Pizzas

Makes 6 pizzas:

12 ounces frozen, fully-cooked chicken fajita strips
6 pita breads
⅔ cup regular or reduced fat mayonnaise
2 tablespoons pesto sauce (prepared)
1 can artichoke hearts (14 ounce), drained and quartered
1 jar or can sliced mushrooms (6 ounces), drained
1 small red bell pepper
2 cups shredded pizza cheese blend

Prep Time: 15 minutes
Cooking Time: 15–20 minutes

Preheat oven to 450°F. Arrange 2 oven racks in bottom half of oven. Cover 2 large baking sheets with foil. Place 3 pitas on each baking sheet.

Microwave fajitas according to cooking instructions and chop into bite-sized pieces.

In a small bowl, mix together mayonnaise and pesto. Evenly distribute mayonnaise-pesto sauce over each pitas.

Arrange chicken, artichoke hearts, and mushrooms over pesto, evenly. Wash bell pepper, remove seeds, and slice into thin strips. Place bell pepper strips over top of pitas with ⅓ cup cheese over each.

Bake 15–20 minutes, or until cheese melts. Switch pans on oven racks halfway through baking for even browning. Allow to cool for a few minutes, slice, and serve.

Side Dishes

Side dishes, like superheroes' sidekicks, do a lot of the unsung work in a meal. They assist a meal's champion, its main dish, by providing additional nutrients and delicious complementary flavors and textures. The recipes featured here are vegetable sides. Some, like Fiesta Corn Salad (page 71), lend a cool, tangy crunch; while others, like Spicy Mashed Potatoes (page 74), are quintessential comfort food—warm and creamy. All are familiar and classic accompaniments to one or more of our meaty main course dishes.

Coleslaw

Serves 6–8:

1 yellow, orange, or red bell pepper
½ small red onion
16 ounces refrigerated coleslaw
2 cups shredded carrots
½ cup golden raisins

Dressing:
⅓ cup apple cider vinegar
3 tablespoons honey
2 tablespoons vegetable oil
2 teaspoons fresh lemon juice
½ teaspoon salt (preferably kosher or sea)
½ teaspoon freshly ground black pepper

Prep Time: 10 minutes

Cut bell pepper and onion into ¼-inch-thick strips.

In a medium bowl, whisk dressing ingredients together.

Combine coleslaw, bell pepper, onion, carrots, and raisins with dressing in a large bowl. Cover and chill 30 minutes before serving, if time allows.

Serves 4:

1 tablespoon butter
1 can diced green chiles (7 ounces)
½ cup chopped onion
1 bag frozen corn kernels (16 ounces)
½ cup shredded Monterey Jack cheese
½ cup sour cream
Salt (preferably kosher or sea), to taste
Freshly ground black pepper, to taste

Prep Time: 5 minutes
Cooking Time: 10 minutes

In a large skillet over medium heat, melt butter and sauté chiles and onion for 3 minutes. Add corn and cheese and mix. Heat for 5 minutes or until corn is hot and cheese is melted.

Add and mix in sour cream right before serving. Season to taste with salt and pepper. Serve hot.

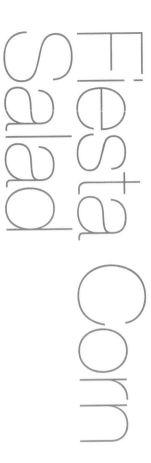

Fiesta Corn Salad

Down Home Potato Salad

Serves 6–8:

2–3 pounds gold or white potatoes
3 hard-boiled eggs
½ cup finely chopped celery
¼ cup finely chopped dill pickle
Dressing:
¾ cup mayonnaise
2 teaspoons spicy brown or stone-ground mustard
1 teaspoon salt (preferably kosher or sea)
½ teaspoon freshly ground black pepper

Prep Time: 15 minutes
Cooking Time: 20–30 minutes

Wash potatoes and peel. Chop potatoes into ½-inch or bite-sized pieces. In a 6-quart pot, add potatoes and cover with water, bringing to a boil. Heat over medium heat for 20–30 minutes or until soft, uncovered.

Drain potatoes, let stand 10–15 minutes to drain well, and cool slightly.

Peel and chop eggs, celery, and pickle. Combine dressing ingredients in a small bowl.

In a large serving bowl, combine potatoes, eggs, celery, and pickle. Combine dressing to potato mixture, coating evenly. Serve salad warm or refrigerate and serve chilled.

Serves 4–6:

1 small bell pepper
4 cloves garlic
1½ tablespoons oil
1 cup chopped yellow or white onion
1½ cups long-grain white rice
1 can diced tomatoes and green chiles (10 ounces), mild or hot
1 can chicken broth (14½ ounces)
Salt (preferably kosher or sea), to taste

Prep Time: 10 minutes
Cooking Time: 30 minutes

Wash, remove seeds and stems, and chop bell pepper. Mince garlic to a very fine consistency.

In a large skillet, heat oil over medium heat. Add onion, bell pepper, and garlic to skillet and sauté for 3 minutes. Add rice and sauté for an additional 5 minutes, stirring often.

Add tomatoes with green chiles, chicken broth, and ½ cup water. Bring rice to a boil, stirring often, reduce heat to low, and cover skillet. Simmer for 15–20 minutes or until liquid is absorbed. Remove skillet from heat source, let stand for 5 minutes, and serve.

Mexican Rice

Spicy Mashed Potatoes

Serves 4:

2–3 individual canned chipotle peppers in adobo sauce
3 tablespoons butter
1 package country-style mashed potatoes (20 ounces; packaged)
2–4 tablespoons milk
1 cup shredded white cheddar cheese
Salt (preferably kosher or sea), to taste
White ground pepper, to taste

Prep Time: 10 minutes
Cooking Time: 10 minutes

Depending on how spicy you'd like the potatoes, finely chop 2–3 chipotle peppers and set aside.

In a 3-quart saucepan over medium heat, melt butter. Add potatoes, chipotle peppers, and 2 tablespoons of milk. Heat well and continue stirring potato mixture. Add cheese to mixture, continuing to stir until cheese is melted.

If desired, add 1–2 tablespoons of additional milk, if potatoes are too thick. Serve hot.

Fruit Salad

Serves 4–6:

2 cups sliced jicama (see cutting instructions below)
2 large navel oranges
1 red bell pepper, cut into thin strips
2 tablespoons chopped fresh cilantro
2 tablespoons brown sugar
1 tablespoon fresh-squeezed lemon juice
Watercress or torn romaine lettuce (optional)

Prep Time: 10 minutes

Peel jicama. Cut into ¼-inch-thick slices, then stack slices, and cut into ¼-inch-wide by 2-inch-long strips. In a medium bowl, add jicama.

Remove peel and white pith from oranges with a sharp knife. Cut orange sections from between membranes and place into same bowl with jicama, holding oranges over bowl to catch any juices from the oranges. Squeeze orange membranes into bowl for additional juice.

Wash, remove stem and seeds, and cut bell pepper into thin strips.

In the same bowl with jicama-orange, combine bell pepper, cilantro, brown sugar, and lemon juice. Toss to evenly coat.

Let flavors meld for 5–10 minutes before serving or chill for 30 minutes, if time allows. Serve salad over torn lettuce leaves.

Serves 4:

10 ounces frozen spinach, thawed and chopped
2 tablespoons butter
2 tablespoons flour
¼ cup finely chopped onion
1¼ cups milk
¼ teaspoon salt (preferably kosher or sea)
Freshly ground black pepper
Pinch of nutmeg

Prep Time: 5 minutes
Cooking Time: 15 minutes

Let spinach thaw overnight in refrigerator or in a colander under cool running water. Drain spinach well, squeezing excess moisture, and set aside.

In a small saucepan, melt butter over medium heat. Add flour, stirring into butter until consistency is smooth. Add onion and sauté for an additional 2 more minutes or until tender.

Whisk milk into onion mixture until consistency is smooth and heated through. Add spinach and stir to blend mixture. Season with salt, pepper, and a pinch of nutmeg to taste. Cover pan, reduce heat to low, and simmer for 5 minutes, stirring occasionally. Serve hot.

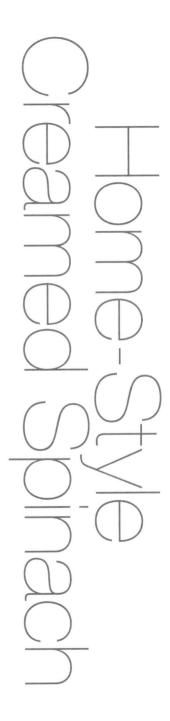

Home-Style Creamed Spinach

Main Meals

In this, our most extensive section, variety stars. We offer a wide selection of main course dishes, featuring an equally wide range of fresh, healthful ingredients from diverse ethnic menus. Using a variety of prepared meats, you can prepare entrée after applause-worthy entrée. Choose from simple, hearty ranch-style casseroles to meaty Mediterranean pastas, from savory curry dishes to traditional Tex-Mex entrées, and from saucy Asian fare to chuckwagon skillet dinners. Variety is the spice of down-home cooking.

Penne with Chicken and Basil

Serves 4–6:

12 ounces frozen, fully-cooked beef fajita strips
12 ounces penne rigate pasta (about 4 cups dry)
1 large onion
1 large red bell pepper
2 cloves garlic
8–10 large leaves fresh basil
1 jar julienne cut sun-dried tomatoes in oil (8 ounces)
½ cup shredded Parmesan cheese

Prep Time: 15 minutes
Cooking Time: 20 minutes

In a 5-quart pot, boil 3 quarts of water. Cook pasta according to package directions. Drain pasta and reserve.

In a microwaveable bowl, heat fajitas according to package directions. Peel onion and slice into thin strips. Wash bell pepper, remove seeds and stem, and slice into thin strips. Mince garlic. Wash basil, remove leaves and discard stems, and cut into thin slices.

Drain oil from sun-dried tomatoes and add oil to a large skillet. Heat skillet over medium heat for 3 minutes. Add onion, bell pepper, and garlic. Sauté vegetables for 8–10 minutes or until onion is translucent. Add sun-dried tomatoes and beef to skillet. Continue to stir to evenly cook all ingredients, about 6–8 minutes.

Combine pasta with beef mixture in a large serving bowl. Sprinkle with Parmesan, basil, and serve.

Serves 12–16:

1 medium onion
4 cloves garlic
2 tablespoons chopped fresh rosemary
2 tablespoons butter
12 ounces sliced portabella mushrooms
1 can condensed beef broth, (10½ ounces)
1¼ cups dry red wine
⅔ cup frozen cranberry juice concentrate, thawed
¼ cup flour
1 cup dried cranberries
3–4 pounds fully-cooked brisket
Heavy-duty aluminum foil

Prep Time: 20 minutes
Heating Time: 40–45 minutes

Preheat oven to 350°F.

Peel onion and garlic and chop both. Wash rosemary, remove leaves and discard stems, and chop.

In a large skillet, melt butter over medium heat. Add onion, garlic, rosemary, and mushrooms. Sauté for 5–7 minutes or until mushrooms are tender.

Combine beef broth, red wine, cranberry concentrate, and flour in a 3-quart saucepan, using a wire whisk to blend. Stir mushroom mixture and dried cranberries into sauce. Bring to a boil and heat sauce until thickened. Remove from heat source and set aside.

Trim fat from brisket and cut brisket across the grain into ¼-inch-thick slices. Tear a large enough piece of foil to wrap around brisket and place it on a baking sheet. Place brisket slices on the foil of the baking sheet, separating slices slightly to pour sauce over and between slices. Seal foil tightly.

Cook brisket in oven 40–45 minutes until heated thoroughly. Serve on a large platter while hot.

Brisket with Rosemary, Mushrooms, and Cranberries

Beef Brisket Casserole

Serves 4–6:

Non-stick cooking spray
1 cup sour cream
16 ounces fully-cooked shredded beef brisket with BBQ sauce
½ cup chopped onion
1 can chopped green chiles (4.5 ounces)
1½ cups fancy shredded Monterey Jack cheese
1 can refrigerated buttermilk biscuits (8-count can)

Prep Time: 10 minutes
Cooking Time: 22 minutes

Preheat oven to 375°F. Spray a 9-inch by 13-inch baking dish with non-stick cooking spray.

Add ½ cup sour cream to shredded brisket in container. Mix together sour cream and brisket and set aside.

In a separate bowl, combine remaining ½ cup sour cream, onion, green chiles, and ¾ cup Jack cheese.

Separate 4 biscuits into 8 halves and place biscuit halves over bottom of baking dish. Spread reserved BBQ beef mixture over biscuits and green chili-cheese mixture. Separate remaining 4 biscuits into 8 halves and arrange over top.

Bake 20 minutes or until biscuits are lightly browned. Remove from oven, sprinkle with remaining ¾ cup cheese, and bake for 2 more minutes or until cheese melts. Let cool a few minutes, cut into squares, and serve.

Cheese-Filled Ravioli with Beef Casserole

Serves 6–8:

12 ounces frozen, fully-cooked Italian-seasoned beef crumbles
Non-stick cooking spray
1 box frozen spinach (10 ounces), thawed and chopped
1 jar puttanesca pasta sauce (26 ounces)
30 ounces frozen cheese-filled ravioli
2 cups shredded mozzarella cheese
⅔ cup grated Parmesan cheese

Prep Time: 10 minutes
Baking Time: 45-50 minutes

Preheat oven to 375°F. Spray a 9-inch by 13-inch baking dish with non-stick cooking spray.

Thraw and drain spinach well, squeezing well to remove moisture.

Coat bottom of baking dish with puttanesca sauce. With about half of the ravioli, arrange ravioli into rows over puttanesca sauce. Arrange spinach and half of ground beef over ravioli. Top with half of mozzarella and Parmesan cheeses.

Arrange remaining ravioli and beef over cheeses. Pour remaining puttanesca sauce evenly over top. Top with remaining cheeses. Cover dish with foil, folding over edges so well sealed.

Bake for 30 minutes. Remove foil and bake for an additional 15–20 minutes or until casserole is heated through. Let cool for 5 minutes and serve.

Serves 4–6:

1 onion
1 can black beans (15 ounces)
1 tablespoon oil
12 ounces frozen, fully-cooked taco or Mexican-seasoned beef crumbles
2 cups frozen corn
1 can diced tomatoes (14½ ounces)
1 can tomato sauce (8 ounces)
1 cup shredded Colby Jack cheese

Topping:
2 large eggs
1 cup milk
1 cup yellow cornmeal
½ teaspoon baking powder
½ cup shredded Colby Jack cheese

Prep Time: 15 minutes
Baking Time: 20 minutes

Preheat oven to 425°F. Peel and chop onion. Rinse and drain black beans.

In a skillet, heat oil over medium-high heat. Add onion and sauté for 3–5 minutes until translucent. Add beef and corn, stirring. Add beans, tomatoes, tomato sauce, and ½ cup of cheese, continuing to stir. Remove beef mixture from heat source, remove, and place in a large baking dish.

In a medium-sized bowl, whisk eggs and milk together. Add cornmeal and baking powder, whisking all ingredients together. Pour topping evenly over beef mixture in the baking dish. Sprinkle top with remaining ½ cup of cheese.

Bake for 20 minutes or until lightly browned. Serve.

Southwest Tamale Pie

Beef Frittata

Serves 4–6:

1½ cups frozen, fully-cooked Italian-seasoned beef crumbles
2 medium red potatoes (about 2 cups)
1 small zucchini
1 small red bell pepper
½ cup finely chopped onion
2 tablespoons olive oil
1 teaspoon salt
1 teaspoon freshly ground black pepper
1 teaspoon dried thyme leaves
1 cup shredded Gruyère cheese
6 large eggs

Prep Time: 15 minutes
Baking Time: 15 minutes

Preheat oven to 425°F. Place oven rack in top third of oven.

Wash potatoes, peel, and dice into ½-inch pieces. Cut zucchini lengthwise into quarters, then crosswise into ¼-inch-thick slices. Wash bell pepper, remove seeds and stem, and cut into ¼-inch pieces.

In a large ovenproof skillet, heat oil over medium-high heat. Add potatoes and onion and sauté for 5 minutes. Add zucchini, bell pepper, salt, pepper, and thyme. Heat for 5 more minutes. Stir in beef and remove from stovetop.

Sprinkle cheese over beef-vegetable mixture in skillet. In a small bowl, beat eggs and pour over top of mixture in skillet.

Bake frittata for 15 minutes, uncovered, until set (when knife inserted in center comes out clean). Let cool for a few minutes, cut into wedges, and serve while hot.

South-of-the Border Casserole

Serves 4–6:

12 ounces frozen, fully-cooked taco or Mexican-seasoned beef crumbles
1 can cream of mushroom soup (10½ ounces)
1 can chunky tomatoes and green chiles (10 ounces)
4½ cups coarsely crushed Doritos (or nacho-cheese flavored tortilla chips)
2 cups shredded Colby Jack cheese

Topping:
1 cup mashed avocado
1 cup sour cream

Prep Time: 10 minutes
Baking Time: 10 minutes

Preheat oven to 375°F.

In a microwaveable dish, cook beef crumbles in microwave according to package directions. In a medium bowl, combine crumbles, soup, and tomatoes with green chiles. In a separate bowl, crush chips coarsely.

Cover the bottom of a 9-inch by 13-inch baking dish with 2 cups of the chips. Layer half the beef mixture over the chips. Top with 1 cup of cheese.

Layer another 2 cups chips over the cheese, and layer remaining beef and cheese. Bake for 10 minutes or until cheese is melted. Remove casserole from the oven.

Spread mashed avocado over hot casserole, add sour cream, and the remaining ½ cup of crushed chips. Cut into squares and serve while hot.

Serves 2–3:

12 ounces frozen, fully-cooked beef fajita strips
Non-stick cooking spray
1 can black beans (15 ounces)
1 can corn kernels (11 ounces)
1 can chopped green chiles (4½ ounces)
8 flour tortillas (6-inch)
1 can enchilada sauce (15 ounces)
2 cups shredded Monterey Jack cheese

Prep Time: 15 minutes
Cooking Time: 12–15 minutes

Preheat oven to 425°F. Spray a large baking sheet with non-stick spray.

In a microwaveable dish, heat fajita strips according to package directions. Chop fajitas into bite-sized pieces.

Rinse and drain black beans and drain corn. In a medium bowl, add beans, corn, and green chiles.

Place 2 tortillas on the baking sheet about 4 inches apart.

Spread about 2 tablespoons of enchilada sauce over each tortilla. Then layer about ¼ cup of fajita pieces and the same amount of bean mixture over the enchilada sauce for each tortilla. Top with ¼ cup of cheese over each top.

Lay a second tortilla over cheese on each stack, then repeat layering process above to complete layers of tortillas and toppings, ending with toppings.

Bake for 12–15 minutes or until tortillas are golden and cheese is melted. Cut into wedges and serve hot.

Enchilada-Style Quesadillas

Pork, Apples, and Sweet Potatoes

Serves 4:

1 large or 2 small sweet potatoes (about 1 pound)
1 medium onion
2 medium tart red apples
2 tablespoons butter
¼ teaspoon salt (preferably kosher or sea)
½ teaspoon freshly ground black pepper
½ teaspoon ground cinnamon
½ cup orange juice
4 pieces frozen, fully-cooked pork chops (bone-in)

Prep Time: 10 minutes
Cooking Time: 20 minutes

Wash and peel sweet potatoes and slice crosswise into ¼-inch-thick pieces. Stack sweet potato pieces and cut into quarters. Peel and chop onion coarsely. Wash apples and remove cores. Cut apple into wedges and cut wedges in half, crosswise.

In a large, deep skillet, melt butter over medium heat. Add potato and onion and sauté for 6−8 minutes. Add apples, sprinkle with salt, pepper, and cinnamon, stirring. Combine all ingredients to coat. Add orange juice and arrange pork chops over the top.

Cover skillet and reduce heat to low and simmer 15 minutes or until potatoes are done and chops are heated thoroughly. Serve hot.

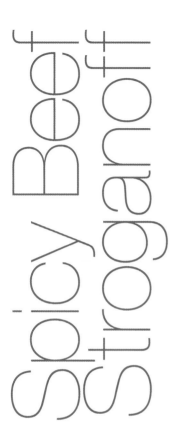

Spicy Beef Stroganoff

Serves 4:

12 ounces frozen, fully-cooked beef fajita strips
Non-stick cooking spray
1 onion
2 small zucchini
1 tablespoon oil
½ cup beef broth
1 teaspoon cornstarch
1 cup chipotle salsa (prepared)
1 cup frozen corn kernels
1 cup sour cream

Prep Time: 10 minutes
Cooking Time: 20 minutes

Cook fajitas, according to package directions and chop into bite-sized pieces.

Peel and chop onion. Cut zucchini lengthwise into quarters and then cut into ¼-inch-thick slices. In a large skillet, heat oil over medium-high heat. Add onion and squash and sauté for 5–7 minutes or until tender.

In a small bowl, stir together broth and cornstarch. Add broth-cornstarch mixture, fajitas, salsa, and corn to skillet. Heat mixture for 2 minutes or until hot and thickened slightly. Stir in sour cream and heat for 5 more minutes. Remove from stovetop and serve hot.

Serves 6:

16 ounces frozen, fully-cooked sliced Philly beefsteak
1 box frozen spinach (10 ounces), thawed and chopped
½ cup cream cheese, softened
⅓ cup sour cream
¼ cup plus 2 tablespoons grated Parmesan cheese
1½ cups pasta sauce with olives
1 cup shredded mozzarella cheese
1 can Pillsbury Refrigerated Crescent Dinner Rolls (8 ounces)

Prep Time: 10 minutes
Baking Time: 20–25 minutes

Preheat oven to 375°F. In a microwaveable bowl, cook Philly beefsteak in microwave according to package directions. Drain any fat from the beef and set aside.

In a colander, drain spinach and squeeze to remove any moisture. In a medium bowl, combine cream cheese and sour cream. Stir in spinach and ¼ cup of Parmesan. Layer spinach mixture evenly over the bottom of a 9-inch by 13-inch baking dish.

Combine reserved beef with pasta sauce and spread evenly over spinach mixture. Top with mozzarella cheese.

Prepare Pillsbury dough by unrolling and place over top of casserole. Sprinkle with 2 tablespoons of Parmesan. Bake 20–25 minutes or until top is golden brown and casserole is cooked through.

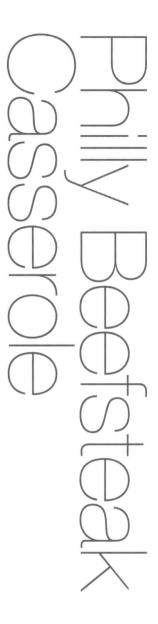

Philly Beefsteak Casserole

Spaghetti Squash with Beef

Serves 4:

1 spaghetti squash (about 2–3 pounds)
1 small onion
1 medium green bell pepper
2 medium tomatoes
12 ounces frozen, fully-cooked beef fajita strips
1 tablespoon olive oil
½ cup grated Parmesan cheese
Salt (preferably kosher or sea), to taste
Freshly ground black pepper, to taste
Garlic powder, to taste

Prep Time: 15 minutes
Cooking Time: 25 minutes

Preheat oven to 350°F.

Using the sharp tip of a knife, pierce squash in 4 places. In a microwaveable dish, heat squash for 8-10 minutes, turning frequently, until tender when pierced with a fork. Chop onion, bell pepper, and tomatoes while squash cooks.

Cut squash in half lengthwise and remove seeds. Using a fork, pull squash from edges into strands that look like strings of spaghetti.

In a microwaveable bowl, heat fajitas according to package directions. Chop fajitas into bite-sized pieces.

In a large skillet, heat oil over medium heat. Add onion and bell pepper and sauté for 5 minutes. Add squash strands, fajitas, and tomatoes. Toss vegetable-fajita mixture to combine. Season to taste with salt, pepper, and garlic powder.

Place squash shells on a baking sheet, cut-sides up. Fill each squash shell with the beef and squash mixture, divided evenly. Spinkle with Parmesan cheese and bake for 10 minutes or until top is lightly browned. Cut each squash half into 2 portions and serve.

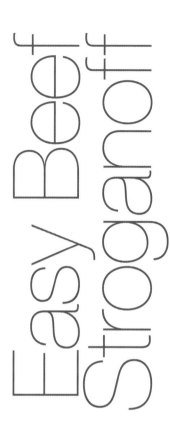

Easy Beef Stroganoff

Serves 4–6:

1 package fully-cooked beef pot roast with gravy (about 1½ pounds)
1 tablespoon oil
1 onion, chopped
8 ounces sliced mushrooms
1 cup sour cream
Salt (preferably kosher or sea)
Freshly ground coarse black pepper

Prep Time: 10 minutes
Cooking Time: 10 minutes

In a large skillet, heat oil over medium-high heat. Add onion and mushrooms and sauté for 5 minutes or until onion is translucent.

From the pot roast package, empty gravy from roast into the skillet. Stir to combine. Lower heat to medium-low and simmer for 5 minutes.

Cut pot roast into ½-inch-thick slices, stack slices, and cut into ½-inch-thick strips.

Add strips to the skillet mixture and cover, heating for 5 minutes or until roast is hot. Stir in sour cream and season to taste with salt and pepper. Serve hot.

Serves 4–6:

1 package fully-cooked beef pot roast with gravy (about 1½ pounds)
16 ounces frozen French-cut green beans
1 can sliced mushrooms (4 ounces), drained
20 ounces refrigerated Simply Potatoes, Country Mashed
¼ cup milk
½ teaspoon salt (preferably kosher or sea)
½ teaspoon freshly ground black pepper
1 can cream of mushroom soup (10½ ounces)
1 can French-fried onions (2.8 ounces)

Prep Time: 10 minutes
Cooking Time: 20 minutes

Preheat oven to 400°F.

In a large microwaveable dish, cook pot roast according to package directions and set aside.

In a colander, place frozen green beans and rinse with cool water to thaw. Drain any moisture from green beans, drain mushrooms, and set aside.

In a medium-sized, microwaveable bowl, heat mashed potatoes according to package directions. Add milk, salt, and pepper to heated potatoes, stirring until well combined and set aside.

Spread reserved pot roast with gravy over bottom of a 9-inch by 13-inch baking dish. Spread reserved green beans and mushrooms over roast. Spread mushroom soup over green beans and mushrooms. Spread reserved mashed potatoes over soup. Sprinkle top with onions.

Cover loosely with aluminum foil and bake for 20 minutes. Serve hot.

Pot Roast and Potato Casserole

Tomato, Squash, and Corn with Pork

Serves 4–6:

2 pounds zucchini or summer squash (about 3 medium)
1 medium onion
1 tablespoon oil
1 teaspoon dried oregano leaves
1 container fully-cooked seasoned pork with juices (16 ounces)
1 can diced tomatoes (14½ ounces)
1 can tomato sauce (8 ounces)
1 can corn kernels (11 ounces), drained

Prep Time: 10 minutes
Cooking Time: 25–30 minutes

Wash squash, trim and discard ends, and cut into ½-inch cubes. Peel and chop onion coarsely.

In a large pot, heat oil over medium-high heat for 2 minutes. Add onion and sauté for 5 minutes. Stir in oregano. Lower heat to medium and let cook for 5 more minutes, stirring frequently.

Add pork with juices, tomatoes, and tomato sauce to pot. Bring to a boil, cover pot, and reduce heat to medium-low. Cook 10–15 minutes or until pork is hot and vegetables are tender

Stir in zucchini and corn and cook for 5 minutes, uncovered. Serve hot.

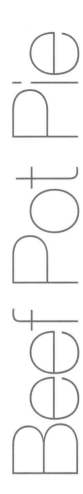
Beef Pot Pie

Serves 6:

1 container fully-cooked shredded pot roast with gravy (16 ounces)
1 package refrigerated pie crusts (15 ounces, two 9-inch)
1 can or jar mushroom gravy (10½ ounces)
1 can chunky style portabella mushrooms (4 ounces), drained
1 box frozen peas and carrots (10 ounces)
1½ cups frozen potatoes with onions and peppers
Salt (preferably kosher or sea), to taste
Freshly ground black pepper, to taste

Prep Time: 10 minutes
Baking Time: 21 minutes

Preheat oven to 450°F. Set pie crusts out and bring to room temperature, according to package directions.

In a large skillet over medium heat, combine mushroom gravy with shredded beef pot roast (including gravy). Add mushrooms, peas and carrots, and potatoes. Season to taste with salt and pepper. Bring to a boil and reduce heat to low, simmering gently.

Unfold one pie crust and place in an ungreased 9-inch glass pie pan. Press crust firmly against sides and bottom of pan and trim crust around edges. If crust cracks, wet fingers and push dough together to seal. Using a fork, prick bottom and sides of crust.

Bake the pie crust for 6–8 minutes, until a light golden brown. Remove from oven and fill crust with pot roast mixture. Place remaining crust over top. Fold back edges of crust and squeeze or crimp with fingers to stand up at outer edge of pan. Cut 4 slits in top crust.

Bake for 15 minutes. Let cool for 5 minutes, slice, and serve.

Serves 4–6:

Casserole:
1 container fully-cooked seasoned shredded beef (12 ounces)
12 corn tortillas
1 red bell pepper
1 can black beans (15 ounces)
12 ounces queso quesadilla or asadero cheese slices (from Mexican grocer and some supermarkets)
1 can chopped green chiles (7 ounces)
Sauce:
1 can green chile enchilada sauce (10 ounces)
1 can salsa verde (tomatillo salsa; 7 ounces)

Prep Time: 15 minutes
Baking Time: 40–45 minutes

Preheat oven to 350°F. Spray a 7-inch by 11-inch baking dish or 2-quart casserole with non-stick cooking spray.

In a microwaveable bowl, heat beef in microwave according to package directions.

Break tortillas into bite-sized pieces or chop coarsely. Wash bell pepper, remove stems and seeds, and chop. Rinse and drain black beans. Pull apart cheese slices. In a small bowl, mix together sauce ingredients and set aside.

CASSEROLE: Layer half of tortilla pieces over bottom of the prepared dish. Arrange half of beef shreds evenly over tortillas along with half of bell pepper, half of black beans, and half of green chiles, all placed over the beef. Spread 1 cup of sauce mixture evenly over top. Arrange half the cheese slices over the sauce in a single layer.

Layer remaining ingredients in the same order as listed above.

Bake 40–45 minutes or until cheese is browned around the edges. Let cool for 5–10 minutes and serve.

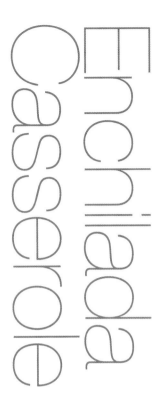

Roast with Port Cherry Sauce

Serves 4:

1 shallot
1 can pitted dark sweet cherries (16 ounces)
½ cup beef broth
⅓ cup ruby port
1 tablespoon tomato paste
1 large fresh bay leaf (optional)
1 teaspoon whole black peppercorns
1 pound fully-cooked beef tenderloin roast (or pot roast)
Salt (preferably kosher or sea)
Freshly ground black pepper
1 tablespoon butter
1 teaspoon cornstarch dissolved in 1 tablespoon water

Prep Time: 10 minutes
Cooking Time: 20 minutes

Peel and thinly slice shallot.

Over a medium saucepan, strain juice from cherries and reserve cherries for later use. Add broth, port, shallot, tomato paste, bay leaf, and peppercorns to cherry juice in the saucepan.

Over medium-high heat, bring cherry sauce to a boil. Lower heat to medium and cook for about 15 minutes, stirring occasionally, until liquid is reduced to about 1 cup and reserve.

Slice roast into ½-inch-thick pieces and set aside.

Over a large skillet on medium heat, strain reduced cherry sauce through a wire mesh sieve. Add butter and cornstarch-water mixture to cherry sauce.

Add reserved beef to the skillet. Heat beef in cherry sauce for about 2 minutes or until sauce thickens. Add reserved cherries and cover skillet, simmering for 1–2 minutes or until well heated. Serve immediately.

Chicken Enchiladas

Serves 4–6:

1 container fully-cooked seasoned shredded chicken (12 ounces)
16 corn tortillas
2 cups shredded cheddar Jack cheese
1 can green enchilada sauce (14½ ounces)
Sour cream, for garnish (optional)

Prep Time: 10 minutes
Baking Time: 20 minutes

Preheat oven to 350°F. Spray a 9-inch by 13-inch baking dish with non-stick cooking spray.

In a microwaveable plate, heat tortillas briefly in the microwave.

Set aside 1½ cups of enchilada sauce for later use as topping. In a small bowl, add remaining enchilada sauce.

Coat both sides of tortilla with enchilada sauce and lay on a flat surface. Add 2–3 tablespoons chicken down center of tortilla and top with cheese. Roll up tortilla and place in the prepared baking dish, seam-side down.

Assemble remaining tortillas as instructed above. Pour reserved enchilada sauce over enchiladas and top with any remaining cheese.

Bake for 20 minutes or until cheese melts and bubbles. Serve with sour cream, if desired.

Serves 4:

1 pound gnocchi pasta
2 pieces frozen, fully-cooked Italian-seasoned chicken breasts
½ cup sliced sun-dried tomatoes in oil, undrained
¼ cup pine nuts
¾ cup chicken broth
1 cup crumbled Gorgonzola cheese
½ cup sliced fresh basil leaves

Prep Time: 10 minutes
Cooking Time: 10 minutes

In a large stockpot, bring 4 quarts water to a boil. When water is boiling, add gnocchi and cook for 3–4 minutes or until gnocchi float to the top. Drain and set aside.

In a microwaveable bowl, heat chicken in microwave according to package directions. Cut chicken into bite-sized pieces and set aside.

In a large skillet over medium heat, add sun-dried tomatoes and pine nuts. Sauté for 3–4 minutes or until nuts are lightly browned. Add chicken broth and cheese, stirring until cheese is melted.

Add reserved chicken and gnocchi, and basil to the skillet. Cook for 2 more minutes or until mixture simmers, stirring frequently.

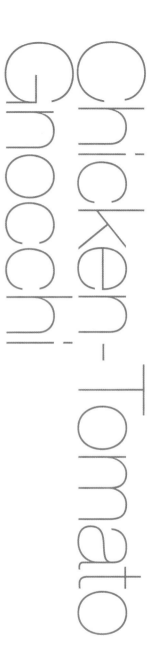

Chicken-Tomato Gnocchi

Chicken Cacciatore

Serves 4–6:

1 onion
1 green bell pepper
2 tablespoons olive oil
1 cup sliced mushrooms
½ cup dry red wine or chicken broth
6 pieces frozen, fully-cooked herb-roasted chicken thighs
1 jar marinara or pasta sauce (26 ounces)
½ cup coarsely chopped kalamata olives, pitted
Salt (preferably kosher or sea), to taste
Freshly ground black pepper, to taste

Prep Time: 10 minutes
Cooking Time: 20 minutes

Peel and chop onion. Wash bell pepper, remove stem and seeds, and chop. In a large, deep skillet over medium heat, add oil. Add onion, bell pepper, and mushrooms. Sauté for 6–8 minutes or until tender.

Add wine or broth and cook for a few minutes. Stir to loosen and combine any browned bits left in bottom of skillet. Arrange frozen chicken in a single layer, meat-sides down in skillet.

Add pasta sauce and olives and bring to a boil. Reduce heat to medium-low and cover and simmer for 10–15 minutes or until chicken is heated thoroughly. Stir occasionally. Season to taste with salt and pepper. Serve.

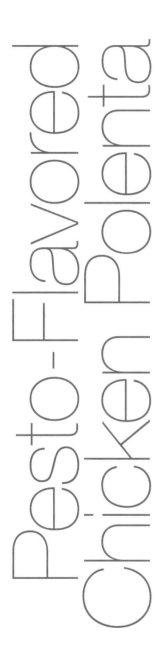

Pesto-Flavored Chicken Polenta

Serves 4:

Polenta:
1 can chicken broth (14 ½ ounces)
1½ cups water
¼ teaspoon salt
1 cup dry polenta or stone-ground cornmeal
½ cup cream or milk
⅓ cup shredded Asiago cheese

2 pieces frozen, fully-cooked pesto- or Italian-seasoned chicken breasts
2 ounces sun-dried tomatoes (dry, not packed in oil)
1 cup white wine
1 medium onion
1 tablespoon olive oil

Prep Time: 15 minutes
Cooking Time: 20 minutes

In a large stockpot, add broth, water, and salt and bring to a boil. Gradually stir in polenta and reduce heat to low and cook for 20 minutes, stirring occasionally.

In a microwaveable bowl, heat chicken in microwave according to package directions. Slice sun-dried tomatoes into very thin strips. In a small bowl, add wine and place sun-dried tomatoes in wine to soften for about 10 minutes. Peel and chop onion.

In a large skillet over medium heat, add oil and sauté onion for 6−8 minutes or until translucent. Add sun-dried tomatoes with wine and stir. Cook for a few minutes or until liquid has reduced by one-half. Remove from heat and cover skillet to keep warm.

Combine cream and cheese with cooked polenta and set aside.

Cut chicken breasts thinly. Place polenta in a serving platter or on individual plates and arrange chicken strips over polenta. Top with onion-tomato mixture, including juices. Serve.

Serves 6–8:

2 onions
2 tablespoons oil
2 teaspoons curry powder
26 ounces frozen, fully-cooked chicken fajita strips
2 cups diced tomatoes (about 2 large tomatoes)
1 can unsweetened coconut milk (14 ounces)
½ cup chopped fresh mint leaves (loosely packed)
1 teaspoon cornstarch
Salt (preferably kosher or sea)
Freshly ground black pepper

Prep Time: 5 minutes
Cooking Time: 30 minutes

Peel and chop onions coarsely.

In a large skillet, heat oil over medium heat. Add onions and sauté for 8–10 minutes or until very soft, stirring often. Add curry powder, stir, and cook for 1 more minute. Add chicken, tomatoes, and coconut milk. Stir and cook for 6–8 minutes or until chicken is well heated.

Dissolve cornstarch in 1 tablespoon water and stir into skillet mixture until thickened. Remove from heat, add mint, and stir. Season with salt and pepper. Serve hot.

Curry, Mint and Coconut Chicken

Asian Stir-Fry with Plum Sauce

Serves 4:

12 ounces frozen, fully-cooked breaded chicken breast nuggets
3–4 cups bok choy (about ½ head)
1 onion
1 red bell pepper
1 tablespoon grated fresh gingerroot
1 tablespoon oil
½ teaspoon crushed red pepper flakes
½ cup dry sherry

Plum sauce:
1 cup condensed chicken broth
1 tablespoon cornstarch
⅓ cup plum sauce
1 tablespoon soy sauce

Prep Time: 10 minutes
Cooking Time: 10 minutes

Preheat oven to 400°F. Line a large baking sheet with foil and arrange chicken chunks on the sheet. Heat chicken according to package directions.

Cut leaves from bok choy stems. Stack leaves, roll up, and slice very thinly to make about 1 cup and set aside. Then, slice bok choy stems thinly to make about 2½ cups. Peel and chop onion. Wash bell pepper, remove stem and seeds, and chop into 1-inch chunks.

In a large, non-stick skillet over high heat, add oil and stir-fry bok choy stems, onion, and bell pepper for 2–4 minutes or until crisp-tender. Add gingerroot and red pepper flakes and cook briefly. Add sherry, stir, and cook a few more minutes, until sherry is almost evaporated.

PLUM SAUCE: Combine broth and cornstarch and stir into skillet mixture until thickened. Add plum sauce, soy sauce, and bok choy leaves. Stir in chicken and let heat through. Serve hot.

Spicy One-Dish Chicken

Serves 4:

12 ounces frozen, fully-cooked chicken fajita strips
1 can Rotel Festival Diced Tomatoes with Lime Juice and Cilantro (10 ounces)
¾ cup water
1½ cups frozen fiesta-style corn
1 can black beans (15 ounces), rinsed and drained
1 box Uncle Ben's Mexican Fiesta Rice mix (6 ounces)
1 cup shredded cheddar Jack jalapeño cheese

Prep Time: 5 minutes
Cooking Time: 15 minutes

In a deep, large skillet, add tomatoes, water, corn, and black beans. Over medium-high heat, bring tomato mixture to a boil. Stir in rice and contents of seasoning packet.

Reduce heat to low and cover skillet tightly. Let simmer for 10 minutes or until most of the liquid has absorbed, stirring frequently. Remove skillet from stovetop.

In a microwaveable dish, microwave chicken according to package directions.

Arrange chicken over cooked rice and sprinkle with cheese. Cover and let stand for 5 minutes or until cheese is melted. Serve.

Serves 4:

2 cups uncooked orecchiette pasta
12 ounces frozen, fully-cooked breaded chicken breast nuggets
1 tomato
½ cup chopped green onions (with white part)
¼ cup chopped kalamata olives
½ cup shredded Romano cheese
Dressing:
2 tablespoons olive oil
1 tablespoon fresh lemon juice
¼ teaspoon coarsely ground black pepper

Prep Time: 10 minutes
Cooking Time: 10 minutes

In a large stockpot, bring 3 quarts water to a rapid boil. Add pasta to boiling water and cook according to package directions. Drain well and set aside.

In a microwaveable dish, heat chicken in microwave according to package directions. Chop chicken chunks into quarters, set aside, and keep warm.

Wash and dice tomato.

In a large bowl, whisk dressing ingredients together. Add hot, drained pasta and toss to coat. Add chicken chunks, tomato, green onions, olives, and cheese. Toss to combine and serve warm.

Szechwan Stir-Fry

Serves 4:

11 ounces frozen, fully-cooked Szechwan chicken breast tenderloins (about 10–12 pieces)
12–16 ounces fresh vegetables
1 tablespoon vegetable oil
1 cup plus 2 tablespoons chicken broth
¼ cup hoisin sauce
1 tablespoon soy sauce
2 teaspoons cornstarch
1 teaspoon sesame oil

Prep Time: 5 minutes
Cooking Time: 10 minutes

In a microwaveable dish, heat chicken in microwave according to package directions.

In a large, non-stick skillet or wok, add oil over medium-heat heat. Tilt skillet or wok to coat bottom. Add vegetables and stir-fry for 3–5 minutes, until just crisp-tender. Remove vegetables from skillet or wok to a bowl and cover to keep warm.

Add 1 cup of broth, hoisin sauce, and soy sauce into skillet or wok, stir, and bring to a boil. Combine chicken, reduce heat to medium, and simmer for 2 minutes.

In a small bowl, combine cornstarch with 2 tablespoons broth and dissolve. Add cornstarch solution and sesame oil to skillet and stir to blend until sauce thickens. Add reserved vegetables back to skillet, toss ingredients together, and serve.

Pork with Cornbread Rolls

Serves 4:

1 container fully-cooked seasoned pork with juices (16 ounces)
1 can yellow hominy (16 ounces)
1 can diced tomatoes with green chiles (10 ounces)
1 can sliced black olives (2.25 ounces)
1 cup Colby Jack cheese
1 tube refrigerated Pillsbury Cornbread Twists (11.5 ounces)
Chopped cilantro or sliced green onions tops, for garnish (optional)

Prep Time: 10 minutes
Baking Time: 20 minutes

Preheat oven to 400F°

Cook pork in the microwave or on the stovetop according to package directions. Stir and break up pork cubes with edge of spoon. Drain hominy, tomatoes, and olives. Combine hominy, tomatoes, and olives with pork. Arrange mixture evenly in a round baking dish or pie pan. Top with cheese.

Take out cornbread twists, but do not unroll dough. Pull dough apart at perforations into 8 rolls. Arrange rolls over top of casserole, pinwheel-style, arranging 7 in a circle and 1 in the center.

Bake casserole for 6–8 minutes or until tops of rolls begin to brown. Turn corn rolls over and bake casserole for 15 minutes more minutes. Garnish with chopped cilantro or sliced green onion tops, if desired.